JUSTIN BIEBER 3D: THE 100% UNOFFICIAL BIOGRAPHY

A BANTAM BOOK 978 0 857 51060 0

First published in Great Britain by Bantam,
an imprint of Random House Children's Books
A Random House Group Company

Bantam edition published 2011

1 3 5 7 9 10 8 6 4 2

Text copyright © Bantam Books, 2011

Design by Shubrook Bros. Creative
www.shubrookbros.com

With special thanks to Louise Grosart, Rhys Willson, Natalie Barnes and Ellie Farmer

Image copyright: Front cover © Contour Images/Getty Images; Back cover: © Startraks/Rex Features, Endpapers all: (TL) © BDG/Rex Features, (TML) © Getty Images, (TM) © Startraks Photo/Rex Features, (TMR) © Kevin Winter/Getty Images, (TRR) © Jason Merritt/Getty Images, (M) © Peter Brooker/Rex Features, (MR) © Gustavo Caballero/Getty Images, (MRR) © BCUPHOTOBANK/Rex Features, (BL) © Jason Merritt/Getty Images, (BM) © Sipa Press/Rex Features, (BMR) © AFP/Getty Images, (BRR) © Greg Allen/Rex Features, Interior photos: pg5 (main) © John Parra/Wire Image/Getty Images, pg6-7 (for inserts see relevant pages), pg8 (main) © Most Wanted/Rex Features, pg9 (main) © Michael Caulfield/AMA2010/ Getty Images, pg10 (TL) © Sipa Press / Rex Features, (ML) © Kevin Mazur/Wire Image/Getty Images (BL) © Kevin Mazur/Wire Image/Getty Images, pg11 (main) © NBCUPHOTOBANK/Rex Features, pg12 © Sipa Press/Rex Features, pg13 (main) © Kevin Winter/Getty Images, pg14 (main) © Canadian Press/Rex Features, pg15 (T) © Francis Dean/Rex Features, (B) © Jason Merritt/Getty Images, pg16 © Sipa Press/Rex Features, pg17 (main) © Peter Brooker/ Rex Features, (BR) © Canadian Press/Rex Features, pg18 (main) © Matt Baron/BEI/Rex Features, (BL) © Startraks Photo/Rex Features, pg19 (T) © Charles Sykes/Rex/Rex Features, (MT) © Startraks Photo/Rex Features, (ML) © Chris Polk KCA2010/Getty Images, (MR) © Tiffany Rose/Getty Images, (BR) © Kevin Winter /AMA2010/Getty Images, pg20 © (main) Startraks Photo/Rex Features (TR)© Steve Meddle/Rex Features, pg21(TL) © Startraks Photo/Rex Features, (TR) © Kevin Mazur/Wire Image/Getty Images, (M) © Brian J. Ritchie/Rex Features, (MR) ©Jeff Kravitz/AMA2010/FilmMagic/Getty Images2743, pg22-23 (main) © Taylor Hill/Wire Image/ Getty Images, (M) © Startraks Photo/Rex Features, (BL) © Comstock, (BR) © Getty Images, pg24 (BL) © Jun Sato/Wire Image/ Getty Images, (R) © MarkVon Holden/Wire Image/Getty Images, pg25 (R) © Jon Kopaloff/FilmMagic/Getty Images, (L) © Jeff Kravitz/AMA2010/FilmMagic/Getty Images, pg26 (main) © Jun Sato/Wire Image/Getty Images, (BL) © Mark Campbell/Rex Features, pg27 (main) © Michael Tran/FilmMagic/Getty Images, (BL) © Carlos Alvarez/Getty Images, pg28 (main) © Flanigan/FilmMagic/Getty Images, (MR) © Michael Caulfield/AMA2010/Getty Images & © David Fisher/Rex Features, (BR) © ITV/Rex Features & © BDG/Rex Features, pg29 (TL) © Startraks Photo/Rex Features & © Moses Robinson/Stringer/Getty Images, (TR) © David Fisher/Rex Features & © Agencia EFE/Rex Features, (ML) © Richard Gardner/Rex Features & © C Flanigan/FilmMagic/Getty Images, (BL) © Carlos Alvarez/Getty Images, (MR) © MarkVon Holden / WireImage/Getty Images & © Kevin Mazur/Wire Image/Getty Images, (BL) © Most Wanted/Rex Features & © Startraks Photo/Rex Features, (BR) © Copetti/Photofab/Rex Features & © Michael Caulfield/AMA2010/ Getty Images, pg30 (main) ©Tod Williamson/Wire Image/Getty Images, (R) © Copetti/Photofab/Rex Features, pg31 (TL) © Sipa Press/Rex Features, (M) © Startraks Photo/Rex Features, (R) © Rex Gregory Pace/BEI/Rex Features, pg32-33 (main) © Startraks Photo/Rex Features, pg34-35 © Startraks Photo/Rex Features, pg36 © Sipa Press/Rex Features, pg37 © Sipa Press/Rex Features, pg38-39 © Jason Merritt/Getty Images, pg40 (main) © Picture Perfect/Rex Features, (R) © Picture Perfect/Rex Features, pg41 (R) © Picture Perfect/Rex Features, (L) © Picture Perfect/Rex Features, pg42-43 © Kevin Mazur/Wire Image/Getty Images, pg44-45 © Startraks Photo/Rex Features, pg46 (main) © Picture Perfect/Rex Features, (L) © KeystoneUSA-ZUMA/ Rex Features, (BL) © Sipa Press/Rex Features, pg47 (TR) © Kevin Mazur/Wire Image/Getty Images, (TL) © Startraks Photo/Rex Features, (ML) © Startraks Photo/Rex Features, (BL) © Startraks Photo/Rex Features, pg48-49 (main) © Moses Robinson/Stringer/Getty Images, (BL) © Carlos Alvarez/ Getty Images, (TR) © Gustavo Caballero/Getty Images, pg50 (T) © George Gojkovich/Getty Images (B) © 2010 Ferdaus Shamim/Wire Image/Getty Images, pg51 (T) © Larry Marano/Getty Images, (M) © Marc Piasecki/FILMMAGIC/Getty Images, (BL) © Jason LaVeris/FilmMagic/Getty Images, (BM) © Gerardo Mora /Getty Images, (BR) © Dave Benett/Getty Images, pg52 (TL) © Mazur AMA 2010/Wire Image/Getty Images, (BL) © Mazur AMA 2010/ Wire Image/Getty Images, (main) © Matt Stroshane/Getty Images, pg53 (TL) © Brian Rasic/Rex Features, (B) © Ilpo Musto/Rex Features, pg54-55 © Neilson Barnard/Stringer/Getty Images, pg56-57 (TL) © Noel Vasquez/Getty Images, (M) © Noel Vasquez/Getty Images, (BL) © Noel Vasquez/Getty Images, (ML) © Sandra Mu/Getty Images for Tourism NZ, (MMR) © Craig Barritt/Getty Images, (TR) © Ron Vesely/MLB Photos via Getty Images, (MR) © Everett Collection/Rex Features, (BR) © Mike Coppola/Getty Images for NHL, pg58-59 (L) © 2010 Alexander Tamargo/Wire Image/Getty Images, (ML) © Kevin Mazur/Getty Images, (MR) © Raymond Boyd/Michael Ochs Archives/Getty Images, (MT) © Kevin Mazur/Wire Image for Clear Channel/Getty Images, (MB) © Getty Images, (TML)© Jeff Fusco/Getty Images, (TR) © Getty Images, pg60-61 (main) © Gerardo Mora/WireImage/ for NARAS/ Getty Images, (M) © Moses Robinson/Getty Images, (TR) © Frazer Harrison/Getty Images, pg62-63 (main) © Jason Merritt / Getty Images, pg64-65 (L) © Masatoshi Okauchi/Rex Features, (M) © Kevin Mazur / Wire Image / Getty Images, (TM) © Simon Runting/Rex Features, (BR) © Simon Runting/ Rex Features, (R) © Mark Campbell/Rex Features, pg66-67 (M) © Kevin Mazur / Wireimage / Getty Images, (BL) © Owen Sweeney/Rex Features, (BR) © Startraks Photo/Rex Features, pg68-69 © Gustavo Cabellero/Getty Images, pg70 © Sipa Press/Rex Features x2, pg71 (TL) © Dimitrios Kambouris/ WireImage for David Lynch Foundation/Getty Images, (ML) © Kevin Winter/Getty Images, (BL) © Mike Marsland/WireImage/Getty Images, (TR) © Jon Kopaloff/FilmMagic/Getty Images, (MR) © Jon Kopaloff/FilmMagic/Getty Images, (BR) © Charles Eshelman/FilmMagic/Getty Images, pg72-73 (main) © Startraks Photo/Rex Features, pg74-75 (main) © Masatoshi Okauchi/Rex Features, (MR) © Gerardo Mora / Wireimage / Getty Images, pg76-77 (main) © Robyn Beck – AFP/Getty Images

Bantam Books are published by
Random House Children's Books,
61–63 Uxbridge Road, London W5 5SA

www.totallyrandombooks.co.uk

www.kidsatrandomhouse.co.uk

Addresses for companies within The Random House Group Limited can be found at:
www.randomhouse.co.uk/offices.htm

THE RANDOM HOUSE GROUP Limited Reg. No. 954009

A CIP catalogue record for this book is available from the British Library

Printed in Italy

THE 100% UNOFFICIAL BIOGRAPHY

JUSTIN 3D
BIEBER

EVIE PARKER

CONTENTS

PAGE
58
BUST-A-GROOVE

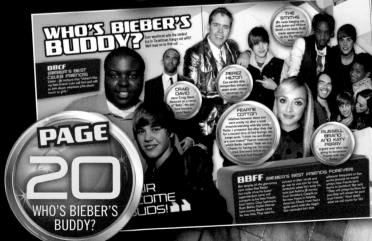

PAGE
20
WHO'S BIEBER'S
BUDDY?

LOVE ACTUALLY?

CHERYL COLE

KATY PERRY

"HE DOES LOVE THE ENGLISH ACCENT AND ALSO THE ENGLISH GIRLS."

BEYONCÉ

SNAPPED WITH SELENA GOMEZ & JUSTINE VILLEGAS

TINA FEY

MIP AKA MOST IMPORTANT PERSON

PAGE 18 LOVE ACTUALLY

GEEK CHIC STYLE

SMART CASUAL STYLE

STYLE TIP!

STYLE TIP!

MOBILE STYLE ABOUT TOWN

MOBILE STYLE ABOUT TOWN

ACCESSORIES

ACCESSORIES

PAGE 24 STYLE FILE

PAGE 72 BIEBEROGRAPHY

PAGE 32 JUSTIN BIEBER 3D POSTERS

BIEBER 3D POSTERS

STEP IT UP

It's fair to say that JB has got a whole lot of energy and when he's out bustin' the moves on stage it seems that he's looking to catch a high octane adrenaline ride with some extreme sports.

BASKETBALL LEGEND?

SKATER BOY?

BASEBALL HEAD?

BUNGEE JUMPING?

ICE HOCKEY WINNER?

TENNIS CHAMP?

PAGE 56 STEP IT UP

7

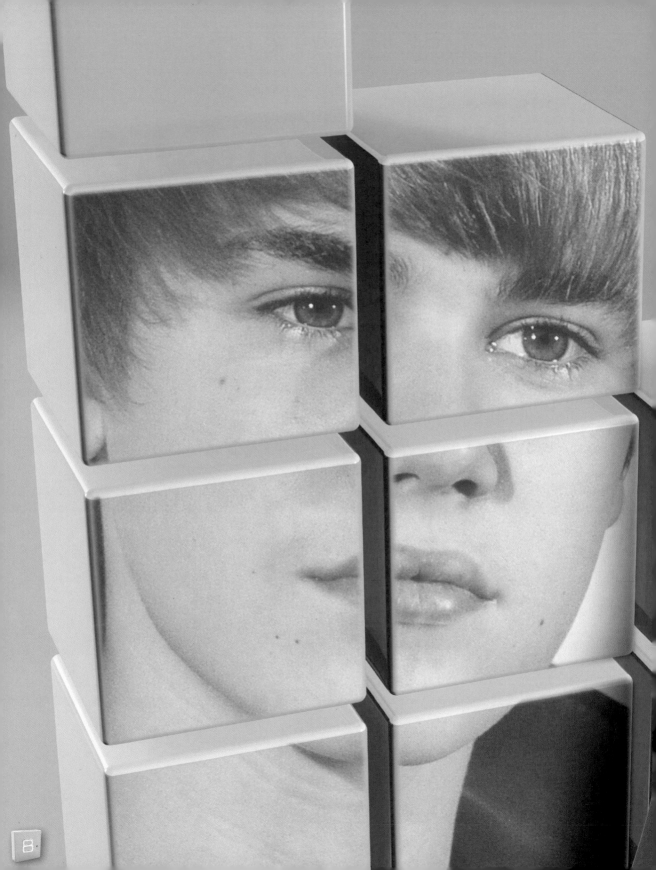

PROFILE

NAME:
Justin Drew Bieber

DATE OF BIRTH:
1 March, 1994

PLACE OF BIRTH:
Ontario, Canada

NATIONALITY:
Canadian

STAR SIGN:
Pisces

HEIGHT:
5'5"

OCCUPATION:
Singer-songwriter

MUSICAL SKILLS:
Vocals, guitar, piano,
percussion, drums, trumpet

MANAGER:
Scooter Braun

SIBLINGS:
A younger sister called
Jazmyn and baby step-
brother called Jaxon

JUSTIN BIEBER:
HIS STORY
ON THE ROAD TO SUPERSTARDOM!

Everyone who's anyone knows who Justin Bieber is. He's the gorgeous, cheeky, shiny-haired pop sensation that's rockin' our – oops, sorry, we mean 'the' – world. And to top it all off, this teen who's loved by girls the planet over is also AMAZINGLY talented. But where did it all begin for this cute Canadian crooner?

Little Bieber!

Talented musician!

Friend and mentor, Usher!

IN THE BEGINNING . . .

JB had always been a talented kid. He grew up in a musical family where his dad played the guitar and his mum sang. He started playing the piano at the age of two and by the age of twelve he'd taught himself how to play the drums, guitar, piano and trumpet!

STREET STYLE . . .

Justin's musical talents didn't go unnoticed around his home town. He famously used to busk outside the town theatre, managing to earn enough money to take the family on their first ever holiday. Chaz Somers' mum remembered first noticing his amazing voice when he sang at the opening of local sports games, but it wasn't until JB came second in a singing contest, and his mum posted the videos on YouTube, that the world started to take notice of this talented youngster.

SPOTTED . . .

Hip-hop producer Scooter Braun was surfing the internet when he found JB's early videos. He instantly knew that the Biebs had some pretty amazing talent and after a bit of detective work, he managed to track down the youngster and invited JB and his mum to visit him at his recording studios in Atlanta, Florida. It was a chance encounter in a car park with R&B legend, Usher, that put JB in the singer's sights. After some negotiating between Island Def Jam Records (Usher's label) and Tennman Records (owned by none other than Justin Timberlake!), JB finally signed with Usher.

10

HE FAMOUSLY USED TO BUSK OUTSIDE THE TOWN THEATRE

JUSTIN BIEBER:
HIS STORY
SIGHTS SET ON THE STARS!

HE'S TOURED THE PLANET, SETTING YOUNG GIRLS' HEARTS A-FLUTTER

Now Justin Bieber is a household name. He's toured the planet, setting young girls' hearts a-flutter in every town, city and state. He's raised money for charity, supported good causes, performed for President Obama, scored countless music award nominations and won a fair few of them, taken over websites, performed on *Saturday Night Live*, duetted with Will Smith's son, Jaden, starred in two episodes of *CSI: Las Vegas* and has had his story made into a 3D movie!

NEXT UP . . .

What will Bieber do next? Will he become a famous sportsman? Perhaps he'll give photography a go. Whatever it is, we know he'll be great. And what makes us say that? Why, because we're true Beliebers, of course! So, please join us in a standing ovation of resounding applause and congratulations for the one and only Justin Bieber. It's his world, and we're happy to be a part of it!

THE BIEBER BIEBLE

OMB! If you're a true Biebette, you'll be fluent in the Bieble. But don't worry if you've still got some phrases to learn — follow our handy guide for all the Bieberisms you need to know!

BELIEBER

Someone who believes in the power of the Bieb.

Example: "I'm a Belieber."

BIEBER-DO
[AKA — THE J-BOB]

Justin's famous haircut.

Example: "I'd like the Bieber-do, please."

BIEBER FEVER

An incurable disease that affects all true/obsessed fans. Symptoms include: screaming, fainting and crying.

Example: "She's suffering from a serious case of Bieber fever."

BIEBERGASTED

When you're so overwhelmed by your love for the Bieber, you can't even string a sentence together.

Example: "I saw him and I was completely Biebergasted!"

BIEBERISH

When you're feeling a bit love sick for the JB.

Example: "Do I have to go to school today? I'm feeling really Bieberish."

BIEBERPHOBIA

A fear of Justin Bieber.

Example: "He can't even put the radio on. He's got Bieberphobia."

BIEBERSTRUCK

When a fan realizes how much they love Justin.

Example: "Mum, I'm totally Biberstruck."

BIEBERTY

When Justin's voice breaks.

Example: "OMB! Justin's hit Bieberty!"

BIEBETTE

A female follower of JB.

Example: "All my best friends are Biebettes."

EAGER BIEBER

A very excited Biebette.

Example: "She's such an eager Bieber, she travelled across the country to see Justin."

HOLY BIEBER!

An exclamation of unbelief.

Example: "Holy Bieber, have you seen Justin's new video!"

NON-BELIEBER

A person to avoid. Someone who doesn't Beliebe.

Example: "Why did he say that about Justin? He's such a non-Belieber."

OJBD

Obsessive Justin Bieber Disorder.

Example: "I'm worried about my little sister. I think she has OJBD."

OMB!

Oh My Bieber!

Example: "OMB! I got tickets to the next Justin concert!!!"

TEAM BIEBER

Only the most loyal Bieber fan can be a member of Team Bieber.

Example: "I'm Team Bieber, all the way!"

WWJBD?

When you're faced with a difficult situation, ask yourself: What would Justin Bieber do?

Example: "Should I go out tonight? Hmmm ... WWJBD?"

15

AND THE WINNER IS...

So, JBiebs may be a winner to all his fans, but what does everyone else think? JB has had a busy few years and we reckon his mantelpiece must be getting pretty full with all the awards he has been winning. Here's just a quick look at the trophies and gongs this chap has scored!

2010 AWARDS

ARTIST – **TRL Award for Best International Act** — WON

ARTIST – **Young Hollywood Award for Newcomer of the Year** — WON

ARTIST – **MuchMusic Video Award for UR Fave: New Artist** — WON

SINGLE 'Baby' – **MuchMusic Video Award for UR Fave: Canadian Video** — WON

SINGLE 'Baby' – **MuchMusic Video Award for International Video of the Year by a Canadian** — WON

ARTIST – **Teen Choice Award for Choice Music: Male Artist** — WON

ARTIST – **Teen Choice Award for Choice Music: Breakout Artist Male** — WON

ARTIST – **Teen Choice Award for Choice Summer Music Star: Male** — WON

ALBUM My World 2.0 – **Teen Choice Award for Choice Music: Pop Album** — WON

SINGLE 'Baby' – **MTV Video Music Award for Best New Artist** — WON

ARTIST – **MTV Video Music Brazil for International Artist** — WON

ARTIST – **Meus Prêmios Nick for Favourite International Artist** — WON

ARTIST – **MTV Europe Music Award for Best Male** — WON

ARTIST – **MTV Europe Music Award for Best Push Act** — WON

ARTIST – **American Music Award for Artist of the Year** — WON

ARTIST – **American Music Award for Favourite Pop/Rock Male Artist** — WON

ARTIST – **American Music Award for T-Mobile Breakthrough Artist** — WON

ALBUM My World 2.0 – **American Music Award for Favourite Pop/Rock Album** — WON

The winner is... **JUSTIN BIEBER**

World Music Awards

VARIETY'S POWER OF YOUTH PHILANTHROPY AWARD

We're pretty sure that JB was well chuffed to have won this mighty accolade for all the good deeds and charitable work he does.

MTV Moonman

GRAMMY AWARDS

He's also bagged two Grammy nominations for Best New Artist and Best Video Performance.

THE 100% UNOFFICIAL BIEBER AWARDS!

Wowzers! What a lot of awards! JB's been a pretty busy guy lately. But we say, why stop there? Here are just a few categories that we think the Biebs would also top if we had any say in the matter.

1 **Best Bob** – OK, we know his hair is already much-talked about and totally legendary, but you know what they say, you can never have too much of a good thing! So Biebs, the Best Bob Award goes to you.

2 **Cheekiest Chat-Up** – JB, for your blatant flirting with Cheryl Cole, we commend you! We just wish it was us you'd asked to call you. We can but dream...

3 **Nicest Guy** – For your work with charity we salute you, sir! You're a heartthrob with a heart!

Biebs busts a groove!

4 **Fabbest Fanbassador** – JB wouldn't be where he is today if it hadn't been for the endless support of his huge fan base. But the best thing about JB is that he knows it, and is always super grateful to all his supporters showing his love for them by tweeting replies, facebooking messages or visiting sick fans in hospital.

5 **Groover** – We don't think he gets praised enough for his awesome shape busting! Biebs, we think you throw some fab dance moves and here's our recognition of it! Best Bust-a-Groove Award goes to you!

17

LOVE ACTUALLY?

Have you got Bieber fever? Yes? Well, we don't blame you, and ladies, you are not alone! Who could resist the charms of this cheeky chappy? Take a look at just a few of the famous gals who have fallen under JB's spell.

CHERYL COLE

Although Biebs has said that he finds England pretty depressing as a country (erm, thanks JB) he's said he does love the English accent and also the English girls! Hooray! And he loved none more than Cheryl Cole. When they met on *The X Factor*, the cheeky young man told her to call him. Well, we don't blame him, she is gorgeous. Sigh . . .

KATY PERRY

Katy Perry has also been pretty vocal abut her celeb crush on JB. The steamy songstress even snuck a kiss from him when they met at the 2010 Kids Choice Awards. She's since said she's over him but Katy, we say once you've gone Biebs, you never go back.

> "CHERYL COLE AND KATY PERRY ARE TWO OF THE HOTTEST GIRLS IN THE WORLD."
>
> – JUSTIN BIEBER

KIM KARDASHIAN

After posing for an *Elle* photoshoot, Justin Bieber admitted he had a crush on the glamorous older lady.

BEYONCÉ

JB's feelings for this lovely lady are legendary. As a kid growing up, JB had posters of her with her Destiny's Child bandmates on his wall and the crush has just stayed. In fact, he's still so smitten he's even admitted that if he could have one wish he'd ask to be handcuffed to Beyoncé for a day – easy tiger!

SNAPPED WITH . . .
SELENA GOMEZ & JASMINE VILLEGAS

Although JBiebs has been linked with these two lovely ladies, he still considers himself a free agent – there's hope for us yet, girls!

TINA FEY

Biebs and funny lady Tina Fey starred in a hilarious sketch on *Saturday Night Live,* but we reckon the chemistry going on there was purely fictional!

MIP AKA MOST IMPORTANT PERSON

But of all the ladies in JB's life, none is more important to him than his mum, Pattie. He says, "She keeps me in line, she keeps me in check and she makes sure I stay humble." Although he's said that spending so much time together can make their relationship fraught, he totally appreciates all the love and support that she provides him with. And when they both need a little time-out, he books her some much-needed spa relaxation – ahh, bless him!

WHO'S BIEBER'S BUDDY?

Ever wondered who the coolest kid in Tinseltown hangs out with? Well, read on to find out . . .

BBCF
(BIEBER'S BEST CELEB FRIENDS)

Usher – JB reckons that "Usher's like my best friend. I can call him and talk to him about whatever. Like about music or girls."

CRAIG DAVID

Since Craig David featured on a remix of 'Baby', the pair have become good pals.

SEAN KINGSTON

News on the street is that JBiebs has been hanging round loads with Sean Kingston – and the pair have become best buds from hooking up at the coolest parties.

THE SMITHS

JB's been hanging out with Jaden and Willow Smith a lot lately. Both made appearances on his My World tour.

PEREZ HILTON

Perez is a massive fan of the Biebs, and we've heard the feeling's mutual.

FEARNE COTTON

Relations between these two were pretty icy after a small misunderstanding with the Radio One presenter, but after they met for a second time all bad feelings were swept aside. "I think me and Bieber are now mates!" Fearne tweeted. To which Biebs replied: "Yeah we are. Thanks for having me. I'm sooo tired. Everyone follow my new best bud Fearne."

RUSSELL BRAND & KATY PERRY

This famous couple argued over who was going to be bestest friends with the Biebs!

BBFF (BIEBER'S BEST FRIENDS FOREVER)

But despite all the glamorous new mates that Biebs has made since he found superstardom, none will ever compare to his best friends from back home. Chaz Somers, Ryan Butler and Nolan Murray have known Biebs since he was little. They take his global success in their stride and go out to visit him for long stretches when he's away on tour. Just before JB moved from Stratford, Canada to his new home in Atlanta, America, Chaz's mum had a quiet word with the singer. She reminded him that whatever happened to him on his popstar journey, he would always have friends back home in Stratford. She said, "They will always be here for you; they will always be your true friends." Now that's what we call mates for life!

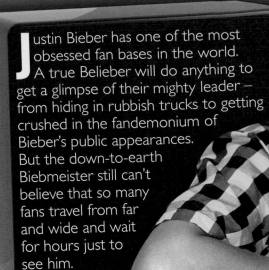

Justin Bieber has one of the most obsessed fan bases in the world. A true Belieber will do anything to get a glimpse of their mighty leader – from hiding in rubbish trucks to getting crushed in the fandemonium of Bieber's public appearances. But the down-to-earth Biebmeister still can't believe that so many fans travel from far and wide and wait for hours just to see him.

FANPU

"I LOVE TOURING AND SEEING MY FANS, I LOVE PERFORMING. I LOVE THE ENERGY AND BEING ABLE TO SING FOR MY FANS."

– JB

THAT'S RUBBISH!

Wonder what weird things his fans get up to? JB said: "The Beliebers have done some pretty crazy stuff. The night before I was due to do a show in Germany, four girls went into a dumpster so they could sneak into the building. They climbed in and hid. When the guys working on the truck started getting the garbage they found them straight away. It was crazy." Fragrant!

Rubbish truck!

CRY BABY BIEBER

Three-year-old Cody became an internet sensation when her sister posted a video of her crying over JB on YouTube. The video has been watched by over two million people, and as it turns out, one of them is Bieber himself.

Jimmy Kimmel flew in the lucky girl and her family to actually meet Justin – maybe we should cry on YouTube too?

FAN FACT

Justin's My World Tour this year will see him visit 85 cities and two million fans!

> "IT'S KIND OF CRAZY THAT MY FANS GET UP SO EARLY TO SEE ME AND THEY ARE OUT THERE SCREAMING. MY FANS DEFINITELY MAKE MY DAY BRIGHTER."
>
> – JB

ASTIC

ASK JB

What's the strangest present a fan's ever given to you?

"A rubber golf club."

THAT'S THE SEGWAY TO DO IT!

Justin has the ability to attract mobs of screaming teenaged girls wherever he goes, but he made a slick (if not rather slow) getaway after a group of fans spotted him in an Arizona car park before a show. As the mass of tweens ran to get a glimpse of the mighty Biebs, he hopped onto a Segway and did his best to evade the Biebettes.

Afterwards on Twitter he told celeb blogger Perez Hilton: "That segway idea almost got me killed! LOL."

JB's fans

STYLE FILE

This rising fashion icon has some serious swagger. With his perfect shiny hair and dazzling smile, he works an urban look and is most often spotted wearing a hooded top or a casual checked shirt. A fashion trendsetter, Biebs doesn't miss a style beat. And here are some of our favourite fashion looks from the megastar cutie.

DAYSTYLE

Justin usually drifts in the direction of a more casual "street" style. A typical daytime outfit for the Biebs is easy to recreate and consists of a pair of slim or straight-leg jeans, a plain T-shirt and either a hoodie or zip-up top. The outfit always includes hi-top sneakers and creates a cool and relaxed look.

Caj hoodie!

MOBILE STYLE ABOUT TOWN!

STYLE TIP!

Bring a flash of colour to your daywear with bright trainers.

ACCESSORIES

Biebs stands out from the casual crowd with his chunky headphones, fingerless gloves, pocket chain, watches and skater sneaks. These well-chosen pieces are a more subtle approach to dressing well.

Bright trainers!

NIGHTSTYLE

This look is a lot more sophisticated and shows more of his fashion creds. He goes for a much darker colour palette in his evening wear, choosing to outfit himself in head-to-toe black. He often dons a blazer, which he dresses around and layers on top of a v-neck or scoop neck tee. JB always likes to feel comfortable – giving him an effortless but sharp look.

Shades at night?!

All black!

STYLE TIP!

Roll up the sleeves of your jacket to really get the chilled-out look that Biebs is famous for.

Rolled-up sleeves!

MOBILE STYLE ABOUT TOWN!

Chain reaction!

ACCESSORIES

Consisting of chains, dogtags, pendants and black sunglasses, JB personlizes his outfits in a fashion-forward way. He's confident with his jewellery and we likie!

Hi-tops!

GEEK CHIC STYLE

Big goggles!

For the ultimate look in Geek Chic, mismatched colours and patterns are the way to go. Justin rocks a checked shirt and more hi-top trainers, giving a nod to the geek within, but keeping firm hold of his cool look and style. He looks like he's just been playing computer games — whilst showing off his creative and fun attitude to his styling.

Checked shirt!

STYLE TIP!

Don't think that Geek Chic equals poorly fitting clothes. Getting the perfect-fit jeans is a must for this look!

Untucked!

MOBILE STYLE ABOUT TOWN!

ACCESSORIES

It's amazing what a difference a pair of thick, black frames can make. But the verdict is still out on the big specs. Do JB's oversized specs = spexy?

More hi-tops!

SMART CAJSTYLE

The military look!

Biebs is the master at mixing high fashion with street-cool. He shows how versatile mixing smart and casual can be by combining and clashing different looks. He never seems to wear smart shoes and wears suit jackets with trainers – adding a bit of flair and reflecting his unique and fun personality.

STYLE TIP!

Team a tailored blazer with skinny jeans to work this look.

Tailored jacket!

Black and white!

MOBILE STYLE ABOUT TOWN!

Skinny jeans!

Shiny shoes!

ACCESSORIES
The Biebs loves his footwear, and keeps it comfortable all the way.

DON'T MESS WITH THE BIEBER BOB?

Those cute, shiny and perfectly swooshed locks have set thousands of Biebette hearts aflutter, but there's a rumour that the Biebs might just be planning a – shock horror – new do!

We've dusted off our snippers and had a go at styling those luscious locks ourselves. Take a look at the eight sleek looks below and argue it out with your mates to see which one you like best.

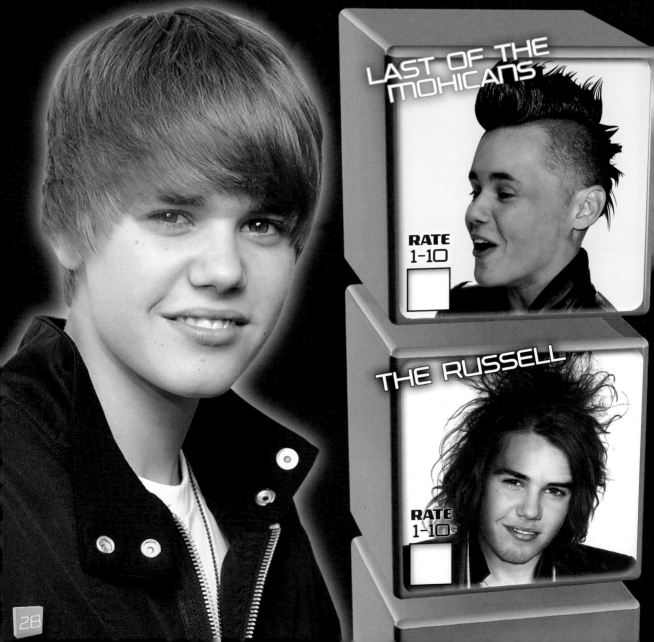

LAST OF THE MOHICANS
RATE
1-10

THE RUSSELL
RATE
1-10

THE ROCK STAR

RATE
1-10

JUSTWARD

RATE
1-10

THE HARRY HILL

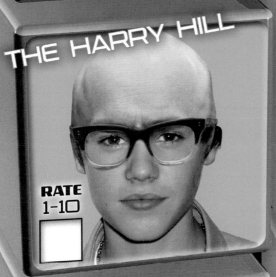

RATE
1-10

DOCTOR WHO

RATE
1-10

THE TWILIGHT

RATE
1-10

THE COWELL

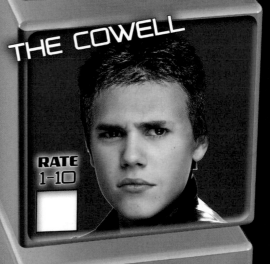

RATE
1-10

SAY WHAT?

Everyone who's anyone has got something to say about the Biebs.
Here are a few of our favourite wise words on the perky pop star.

ALEXANDRA BURKE

"HE'S A NEW GUY THAT'S OUT THERE, DOING HIS THING AND FOLLOWING HIS DREAMS. RESPECT TO HIM."

Respect to you, Alexandra, for having such great taste!

WILL FERRELL

"HE COMES WITH HIS OWN 3D GLASSES. HE LIVES HIS LIFE IN 3D."

Will, so subtle. So funny. So true.

MARK WAHLBERG

"WHATEVER HE WANTS TO DO, AS LONG AS HE STAYS A POSITIVE ROLE MODEL IT'S ALL GOOD. IF NOT, I'LL GIVE HIM A WEDGIE."

Ouch! Better watch out for the Wahlberg Wedgie, Biebs.

SNOOP DOGG

"JUSTIN BIEBER'S ALRIGHT WITH ME, I LIKE HIM."

Now, that that is cool praise indeed. Can we predict a Snoop Dogg/JBiebs collaboration in the future? We certainly hope so.

TAIO CRUZ

"HE'S A VERY COOL KID, VERY TALENTED."

Here, here, Taio!

Never one to let others outdo him, JBiebs has some pretty amazing words of wisdom, too. Here are some corkers that we're very proud to share with you. You go, Biebs!

"IT WOULD BE A SHAME TO GO OUT WITH A HOT GIRL YOU CAN'T HAVE A DECENT CONVERSATION WITH!"

High five to you, JB!

"THERE'S MORE PEOPLE THAT LIKE ME THAN THERE ARE WHO HATE ME, SO I KIND OF BRUSH IT OFF."

Very wise words. Now that's what we call PMA.

"JUST SEEN WILL FERRELL IN A SWEAT SUIT. WHY NOT. WILL IS THE MAN. WILL FERRELL IS THE DUDE! THE MAN HAS SPUNK. PURE SPUNK. HAHA."

True story JB, not many of us can rock a sweat suit.

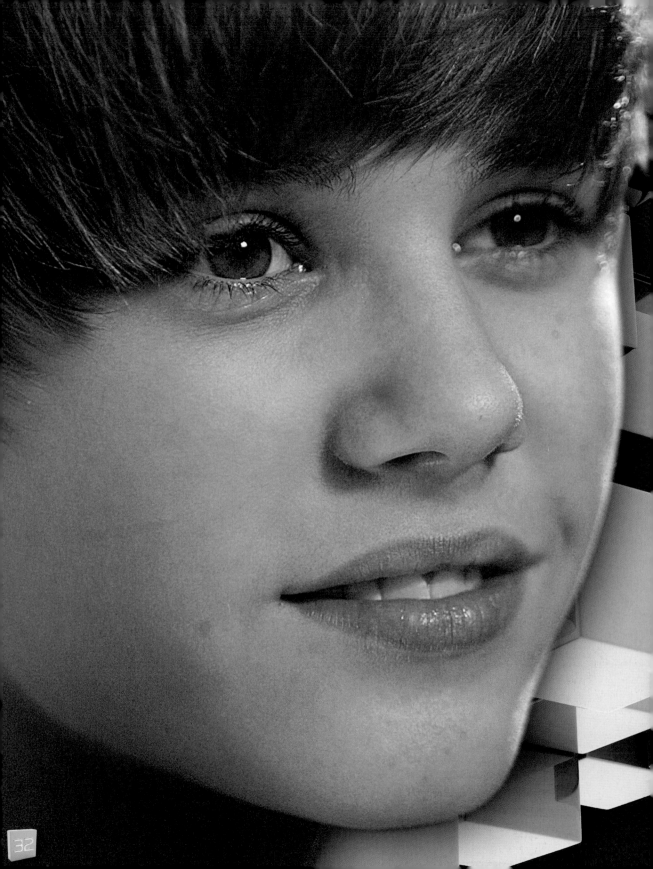

JUSTIN BIEBER 3D POSTERS

JUSTIN BIEBER 3D POSTERS

© Francis Dean/Rex Features.

© Picture Perfect/Rex Features.

© Michael Tran/FilmMagic/Getty Images

© Kevin Mazur/Wire Image/Getty Images

© Jun Sato/Wire Image/Getty Images

© Flanigan/FilmMagic/Getty Images

© Robyn Beck – AFP/Getty Images

© Moses Robinson/Stringer/Getty Images

© Picture Perfect/Rex Features.

© Gustavo Caballero/Getty Images.

© Kevin Mazur / Wireimage / Getty Images.

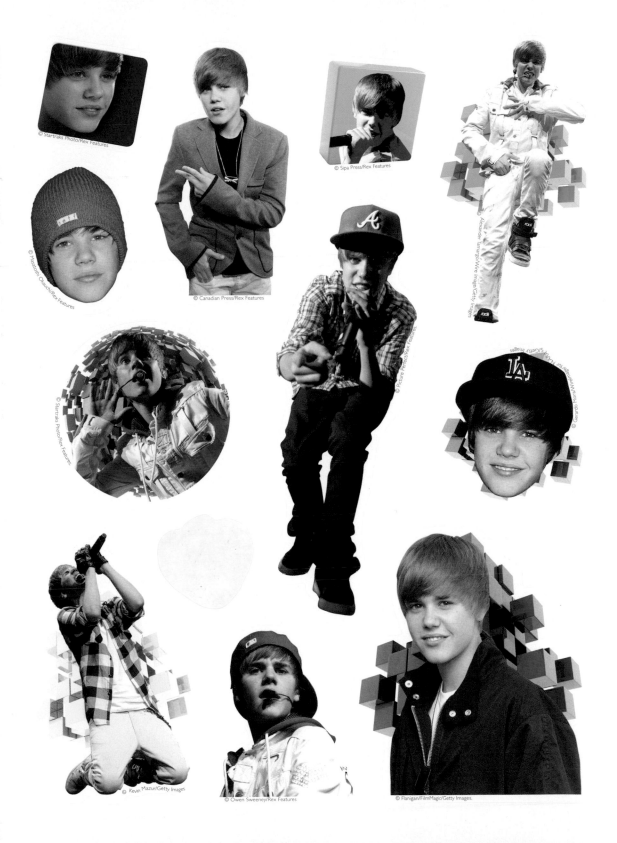

© Startraks Photo/Rex Features

© Sipa Press/Rex Features

© Masatoshi Okauchi/Rex Features

© Canadian Press/Rex Features

© Alexander Tamargo/Wire Image/Getty Images

© Startraks Photo/Rex Features

© Picture Perfect/Rex Features

© General Wallingridge for KAABOO S/Getty Images

© Kevin Mazur/Getty Images

© Owen Sweeney/Rex Features

© Flanigan/FilmMagic/Getty Images.

JUSTIN BIEBER 3D POSTERS

41

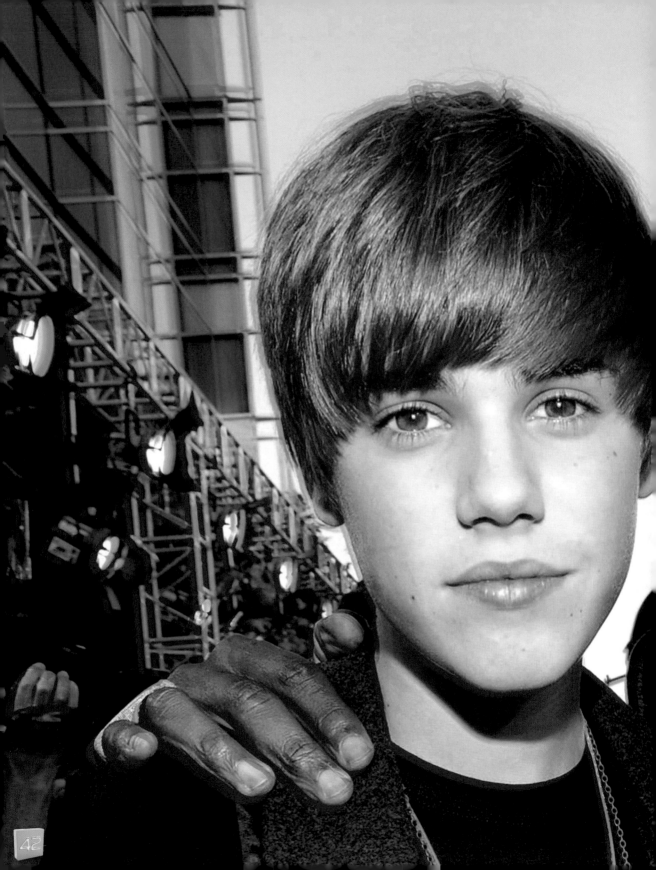

JUSTIN BIEBER
3D POSTERS

43

WORLD TOUR WHIRLWIND

It's been a pretty crazy few years for this kid. For a guy who didn't have the chance to get on a plane before the age of 13, he's certainly made up for it! JB has a truly international fan base, just check out all the jet-setting he's been up to!

THE LANGUAGE OF LOVE
Wanna find out how to say "I love you" to Biebs around world? Here's a few examples:

"JE T'AIME, BIEBS." FRENCH

"TE QUIERO, BIEBS." SPANISH

"WO IE NI, BIEBS."
CHINESE

"ICH LIEBE DIC, BIEBS."
GERMAN

"TI AMO, BIEBS."
ITALIAN

ACCESS ALL AREAS!

What can you expect from a JBiebs concert? Apart from some hot sets from the pop sensation himself, you can guarantee that his support acts are going to be wild! Check out some of the lucky performers who've had the chance to star on stage with the Biebmeister!

SEAN KINGSTON
After supporting the Biebs, now the pair are BFFs round Tinseltown.

JASMINE VILLEGAS
She's got a motion-activated Skittles machine that talks to her!

And if that wasn't exciting enough, check out some of the surprise guests that JB has brought onstage!

USHER – SO COOL
JADEN SMITH – SO KUNG FU
MILEY CYRUS – SO LOVELY
BOYZIIMEN – SO OLD SKOOL
LUDACRIS – SO HOT
SHAQUILLE O'NEAL – SO TALL

VITA CHAMBERS
She was spotted on MySpace.

WILLOW SMITH
JB asked her to support him. Then she joked about whether or not she'd ask her big bro, Jaden, to come along!

IYAZ
He helped the Biebs out when he was being crowded by too many fans and now they're great pals.

THE STUNNERS
These ladies are going to be huge Stateside.

PRANK'D!

Apparently, news on the street is that JB is King of the Pranks and being on tour with him can get pretty wild!

1 Biebs and his entourage race round backstage on Segways!

2 Waterguns are a huge feature of JB's backstage action. If you're into joking, then you'll get a soaking!

3 Burnham filled JB's tour bus with plastic balls and when the star found them he pelted them at the band whilst they were performing their set!

4 Biebs nearly got himself in real trouble when he chucked a water balloon at police officer!

5 His road crew got their own back on the sneaky prankster when they arranged for a hairy, middle-aged biker guy to be on stage whilst JB sung his hit 'One Less Lonely Girl' to him! It was supposed to be a hot chick, poor Biebs!

BIEBER on THE BOX

Justin's not only a musical talent – he's also a TV and film star in the making! He's taken over the radio . . . and now he's going to take over the box.

ON THE TELLY

Bieber made his acting debut on the season opener of *CSI: Crime Scene Investigation*, playing troubled-teen Jason McCann.

The episode, entitled 'Shock Waves', sees the CSI chasing McCann's brother – a bomb suspect.

Behind the scenes, Justin said: "I think the fans will like it. It's going to be fun. It's high energy. I'm playing a character and he's kind of a bad kid.

"Watching *CSI* growing up was really fun for me and my mum. We watched all of them. Now that I'm on it, it's really cool. My favourite part of it was working with George Eads (who plays Nick Stokes), he's really nice and helped me get into the character."

And what did George think of the Biebs? "He's very popular and he's very gifted. I think it will be cool for fans of the show to see him do some acting."

YA KNOW WHAT?!

Justin said the hardest part of acting in *CSI* was remembering the lines!

48

FILM STAR!

What could be better than JB in 3D? Well, apart from having the real thing, obviously! Justin named his documentary *Never Say Never* after his song that featured on *The Karate Kid* soundtrack. The Bieber biopic focuses on his rise to fame and is directed by Jon Chu who directed *Step Up 3D*.

Usher makes an appearance, and we get to see some childhood footage of the ridiculously cute baby Bieber.

Chu told MTV: "It's really an interesting sort of pass between his real life to his music, so I think in the trailer, we break it down every step of the way in his life. Everyone said, 'It's not possible ... Every step?! Everyone's always said, 'No, no, no, no.' And he's always said, 'Yes, yes, yes.' And that sort of 'never say never' idea is conveyed in the trailer."

"ME AND MY MUM WATCHED CSI... NOW I'M ON IT!"

WHAT'S NEXT?
GET YOUR PUNK ON!

Rumour has it that Justin is set to revamp MTV show, *Punk'd*, where he will try to pull off major pranks on unsuspecting celebs. Ashton Kutcher, who hosted the show from 2003-07, will be an executive producer. JB said: "I would love to do it. I'm a prankster. I like to push the limits. I don't know if I'm rebellious, but I like to push the limits."

TOM BRADY

The American football player's long locks have been mocked for resembling the popstar's, and JB rapped online about it! In the video clip, Biebs rhymed: "Sacked like a sacker. Call up Mr. Brady. Tell him to leave his hair to the guy who sings 'Baby.'" Ouchie!

DID YOU KNOW?
JB's alter ego rapper name is none other than ... Shawty Mane!

WANNA

When Justin graduates from the teen throne, who will take his Pop crown? Luckily for us, there are a number of worthy candidates waiting to take his place.

DID YOU KNOW?
Biebs performed 'Baby' and 'Somebody to Love' on X Factor.

ONE DIRECTION

These five *X Factor* hotties are often compared to Biebs. When JB performed on our fave talent show, he showed off his impressive dance moves and reportedly offered the One Direction boys some dance lessons. During an interview on *The Xtra Factor*, band member Zayn Malik said: "I was backstage with Bieber and he said that he was going to give me some dance lessons." Liam Payne added, "Justin Bieber is great – he's a great performer. We just hope we can dance like that one day."

CODY SIMPSON

The Australian pint-sized popstar has been labeled the new Justin Bieber. The 13-year-old has been writing songs since he was seven, and started posting them on YouTube soon after that. It wasn't long before the Aussie cutie was discovered by producer Shawn Campbell, who has worked with everyone from Jay-Z to Ciara.

BIEBS

GREYSON CHANCE

It's not very often that a sixth grade festival performance becomes so crazily viral that it achieves more than eight million YouTube hits in just two weeks. But that's what Greyson Chance's performance of Lady Gaga's 'Paparazzi' achieved, after the 13-year-old uploaded his video.

HAIR WARS

The Bieber-do is side-sweeping the nation! And Biebs is not the only one sporting the helmet-like cut that includes a long, side-swept fringe.

15-year-old Miles Heizer wears his blond hair in the Bieber do for his role on family drama The Parenthood.

The Suite Life of Zack & Cody stars Cole and Dylan Sprouse both traded in their shaggy style for "The Bieber," as well.

Even Ashton Kutcher rocked the shag for a while. Last year he tweeted: "Time for a hair cut. I'm starting to look like Justin Bieber."

AND THE BEAT GOES ON

JB's sound is a funky mix of R&B with some catchy tunes and lyrics thrown in. But don't think that he's just about the amazing vocals. This guy has some serious musical talent up his sleeves and has admitted that he takes his musical influence from loads of places.

PLAY THAT!
Did you know that JB can play the piano, guitar, drums and trumpet!

FAV SONG TO SING?
'You Got it Bad' by Usher

FAV SONG THAT ISN'T R&B?
'Sweet Child o' Mine' by Guns N' Roses

CRIMBO TUNE?

'Rudolph the Red-Nosed Reindeer'

MUSICAL IDOLS?

"I'd like to be a mix between Prince and Michael Jackson."

Tips for YouTube Success?

"IF YOU'RE A SINGER YOU JUST GOTTA PUT IT UP. HOPE FOR THE BEST AND TAG THE VIDEO RIGHT"

What's on his iPod

Usher (obvs!)
Kanye West
Li'l Wayne
Eminem
Drake
Neo
Craig David

DID YOU KNOW?

Justin's song 'Pray' was inspired by his devotion to Michael Jackson's work, in particular, 'Man in the Mirror'.

About Idol, Michael Jackson

"I TOOK IT REAL BAD WHEN MICHAEL JACKSON PASSED. HE WAS AN INSPIRATION TO SO MANY PEOPLE BUT HIS LEGEND LIVES ON. I JUST LOVE HIS MUSIC ALONG WITH OLD SOUL MUSIC."

BIEBER'S BRAIN

The Biebs has got a lot of things on his mind – here's what we think is going on up there.

MY FANS ROCK!

Biebs loves his fans – and we love him back.

12%

MUSIC

The most important thing in Biebs' life – and we don't mind (maybe a little).

44%

HOW MUCH OF YOUR BRAIN IS DEVOTED TO JUSTIN?

Have a chat with your mates and find out what percentage of your brain is dedicated to JB!

.... %

I'M MATES WITH USHER

8%

Only the coolest guy in R'n'B.

DANCING

23%

JBiebs just loves to bust-a-groove.

I WANNA BE AN ACTOR

6%

With his recent stint on *CSI*, we wanna see him more.

I'LL MARRY CHERYL COLE

2%

How much do we wish we were Cheryl right now?

I LOVE TO TWEET!

5%

With millions of followers, who can blame him!

STEP IT UP

It's fair to say that JB has got a whole lot of energy and when he's not bustin' the moves on stage it seems that he's looking to catch a high octane adrenaline ride with some extreme sports.

Jaden Smith!

David Beckham!

Maybe he's a fan of the cheerleaders too?

BASKETBALL LEGEND?

Biebs is renowned for his ball skills and whenever he gets a spare moment, he's admitted that there's nothing he likes better than shooting some hoops. His favourite team is the LA Lakers. He's also a huge fan of BIG basketball legend Shaquille O'Neal!

The Biebs can often be spotted watching his team courtside along with fellow Lakers fans Jaden Smith, Denzel Washington and is that .. . David Beckham?!

BUNGEE JUMPING GURU?

We always knew that JB had his sights set on the heady heights of superstardom, but it seems the teen sensation's love for hitting new highs knows no bounds! When he was visiting New Zealand, the popstar made an epic bungee jump off the Auckland Bridge with his mum and security guard. According to the organisers, JB and his mum had a great time and it was the Biebster's burly security guard who was most worried about taking the plunge!

SKATER BOY?

When Biebs isn't riding his Segway, you'll probably find him speeding down the sidewalk on top of a sleek skateboard.

BASEBALL HEAD?

JB threw out the first pitch at the Chicago White Sox – Kansas City Royals game.

TENNIS CHAMP?

Maybe tennis isn't the game for Biebs?

ICE HOCKEY WINNER?

Coming from Canada, JB is a massive ice hockey fan. He's a huge supporter of the Toronto Maple Leafs and he had the massive honour of getting to hold the prestigious Stanley Cup. This is awarded annually to the National Hockey League (NHL) playoffs champion after the Stanley Cup Finals.

BUST-A-GROOVE

JBiebs is a guy of some seriously smooth moves. Whether he's sashaying down the red carpet, or throwing some shapes live on stage, we think he's got some mighty grooves! Here's our tribute to some of his best — feel free to re-enact them on a dance floor near you!

In Knee-d
D'you see what we did there? Oh yeah!

We like to call this move the Karate Kid.

This one's entitled the Power Grab.

58

There's only one name for this: the **Downright Crazy!**

Whatcha doin' there JB? Oh just a bit of **Toe Poppin'** sweet.

It's the **JB Jump**, obvs!

Jaden and Justin are just **Slippin' Some Skin.**

59

MAKING A
DIFFERENCE

It can't be easy being an international teen sensation, but Justin is doing a pretty good job of keeping his size sevens on the ground. Thanks to a supportive family and tight group of friends, the Biebs is making quite a name for himself in the charity world. Could we love him anymore?

SANTA BIEBER

Who needs to beliebe in Santa Claus when Justin's around? The super-cute pop star teamed up with a local radio station to collect toys for Children's Healthcare of Atlanta while he was on tour in Georgia. Instead of using Santa's sleigh, JB used his tour bus and filled it with toys for every single child at the hospital.

TWITTER DREAMS

Huge JB fan Hayley Okines, a 12-year-old who suffers from the rapid aging disease progeria, was able to meet her hero thanks to the efforts of @BiebsmeetHayley. Justin posed for pictures with Hayley and her family, signed autographs for them and even gave her tickets to his concert in the UK. He also offered free passes to the group responsible for putting him in touch with Hayley.

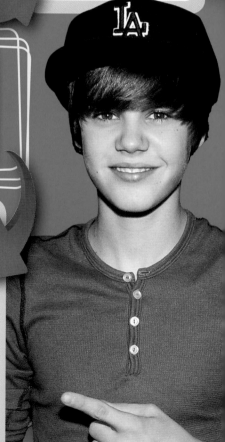

twitter

Bieber tweeted:
Every child deserves a toy this holiday season. Let's make sure these kids in the hospitals have a smile on their face.

twitter

Bieber tweeted:
U did a good thing. And you were right she has a great smile. It was actually kinda funny. She had no clue and when she saw me she screamed and everyone was like what the?!?! She was real sweet and I offered her tix for the show in the UK when I'm back. I think you should go with her then too… The fans did a good thing. Glad I could help. Thanks for introducing us. She is a sweet girl.

"I THINK THAT IT DOESN'T REALLY MATTER WHAT YOU DO. AS LONG AS YOU'RE HELPING OTHER PEOPLE, WHY NOT DO IT?"

"JUSTIN REALIZES THAT IF HE GROWS UP TO BE A GOOD MAN, HE'S GOING TO BE ABLE TO HANDLE THE PRESSURES THAT COME WITH A POSITION LIKE THIS."

SCOOTER BRAUN
(JB'S MANAGER)

"WE CAN ALL MAKE A DIFFERENCE."

Here are just a few more of the wonderful things that the Biebs has done to make a difference . . .

- Justin performed on a Canadian charity version of K'naan's 'Wavin' Flag' which featured artists from Bieber to Drake to Nelly Furtado, and managed to pull in over $1 million for Haiti relief.

- Justin teamed up with charity Children's Miracle Network to launch the fundraising campaign, where he donated a portion of proceeds from the sales of My World Acoustic to children's hospitals in America.

- He is associated with Pencils of Promise — an organisation that works with local communities to build schools and increase educational opportunities around the world.

- A group of JB's fans helped him raise over $200,000 for a children's hospital in Buffalo, New York.

- Biebs was honoured for his good deeds at Variety's 4th Annual Power of Youth event in Hollywood to celebrate the power that kids and teens can have on the world.

- JB presented $32,690 to the Community Foundation of Middle Tennessee's Nashville Flood Fund.

- Justin made a secret visit to London's Great Ormond Street Hospital for Children, and spent time with young patients, many of whom were seriously ill.

FACT OR FICTION?

As the most googled person on the planet, the internet is sure to be full of Bieber fibs! Can you tell which of the statements below are fact and which are fiction?

1 Justin's middle name is Jeremy.

2 Justin doesn't like water, so his entourage play a game to make him drink it. They have a chugging race to see who can drink a bottle of water the quickest.

3 Justin has employed his very own lookalike to help distract attention when he goes out in public.

4 Justin spends between 15 and 20 minutes a day on his hair.

5 JB has asked Justin Timberlake for dating advice.

6 Justin once flashed his abs to Rihanna in the middle of a restaurant.

7 Justin was first spotted by Eminem on YouTube, but his mum wouldn't let them meet.

8 On Justin's first date, he stained his white shirt with a big blob of spaghetti.

FUNNY PHOTOS

JBiebs doesn't just make memorable, awesome music — he sometimes gets caught pulling funny faces and throwing hilarious shapes!

Click, click goes our massive crush on Justin Bieber. An internet sensation, Bieber's huge online fanbase has made him the internet king! Check out these stats!

Justin is the most searched person on the internet

Justin collected 1.07 billion streams through December 2010

"THEY MAKE ME A TRENDING TOPIC ON TWITTER EVERY DAY, IT'S PRETTY INCREDIBLE. I DON'T THINK THERE'S BEEN A DAY IN THE PAST MONTH THAT I HAVEN'T. SO, IT'S PRETTY INCREDIBLE. I LOVE TWITTER."

Justin was ranked second on The Social 50 — a list that ranks artists who get the most plays on social media sites like YouTube, Facebook and Twitter

Justin was discovered on YouTube

THE NET

Justin accounts for 3 percent of all Twitter activity

Justin's 1.07 billion streams in 2010 = incredible 6.9 percent of the 14.8 billion videos streamed by the top five publishers this year. In other words, about one of every 14 streams for the top five publishers was a Bieber video

'Baby' took the number one spot for the most searched lyrics on Yahoo

He has over 16 million fans on Facebook

"I'M ALWAYS ON MY COMPUTER – ON FACEBOOK OR TWITTER. I TWEET MYSELF. I TRY TO REPLY TO AS MANY PEOPLE I CAN. "

He has almost 8 million followers on Twitter

'Baby' featuring Ludacris is YouTube's all-time most viewed video with 405 million streams – and counting

Justin won a new legion of fans online, after a slowed down version of 'U Smile' (slowed by 800%) was posted on the net

GO WITH THE

When it comes to making it big in the world of pop, everyone has their own touch of *The X Factor*. Whether you were made to be a dancer, manager or singer, follow this flow quiz to find out what sort of star you'd be.

START

Your fave tune comes on the radio. Do you:

A. Start dancing?
B. Starting singing?

A

You're happiest when you're:

A. Dancing!
B. Relaxing!

B

B

If there's something to be organised, do you:

A. Jump straight in?
B. Let someone else do it?

A

You'd never leave the house without:

A. Your diary.
B. Your iPod.

A

B

A

When you're out with your friends, are you:

A. Laid back and relaxed?
B. The centre of attention?

B

You're off to a party. You knew what to wear:

A. Three days ago.
B. Just before you left the house.

B

FLOW

Your fave computer game is:

A. Just Dance.
B. Rock Band.

A →

Your pop idol is:

A. Michael Jackson.
B. Justin Timberlake.

A →

DANCER

Wow! You've got an amazing pair of dancing shoes – and you're not afraid to use them! When you hear a beat, you can't help but move those feet!

B

A

B

Your fave clothes are:

A. Joggers and trainers?
B. Caj but cool blazer?

Your friends say you are:

A. Modest and supportive.
B. A bit of a show off, but lots of fun.

A →

MANAGER

You're the person that all your friends can rely on. You've always got their best interests at heart, you're loads of fun, and boy, can you organise a party!

B

A

Someone suggests karaoke. Do you:

A. Cringe!
B. Grab that mic!

A

If someone tells you a secret, you:

A. Keep it to yourself.
B. Tell your BFF cos' that doesn't count.

A

B

You use your mobile for:

A. Talking to your friends.
B. Listening to music.

B →

SINGER

You've got a cracking pair of pipes and the confidence that will get you far. Always believe in your talents and never say never!

69

SPOT THE DIFFERENCE

Polish those peepers and see if you can spot the ten differences between these two Biebertastic pics!

ANSWERS OVER THE PAGE!

IN A SPIN!

These friends of Justin have had their faces warped. Can you tell who's who?

ANSWERS
OVER THE
PAGE!

BIEBEROGRAPHY

MY WORLDS ACOUSTIC 2010

1   One Time [Acoustic Version] (3:06)

2   Baby [Acoustic Version] (3:35)

3   One Less Lonely Girl [Acoustic Version] (3:58)

4   Down to Earth [Acoustic Version] (4:03)

5   U Smile [Acoustic Version] (3:17)

6   Stuck in the Moment [Acoustic Version] (3:19)

7   Favorite Girl [Live] [Acoustic Version] (5:10)

8   That Should Be Me [Acoustic Version] (4:09)

9   Never Say Never [Acoustic Version] (3:43)

10 Pray [Acoustic Version] (3:33)

BIEBER EXTRAS!

In November 2010, the Biebs also released a very special 2-disc double album called My Worlds: The Collection. This featured select songs from My World, My World 2.0 and My Worlds Acoustic, plus, extra songs like 'Common Denominator' and amazing remixes with guest stars including Usher and Jaden Smith!

Justin Bieber

My World

MY WORLD 2.0 2010

1   Baby (3:34)

2   Somebody to Love (3:41)

3   Stuck in the Moment (3:43)

4   U Smile (3:17)

5   Runaway Love (3:33)

6   Never Let You Go (4:24)

7   Overboard (4:11)

8   Eenie Meenie (3:23)

9   Up (3:55)

10 That Should Be Me (3:53)

MY WORLD 2009

1 One Time (3:35)

2 Favorite Girl (4:16)

3 Down to Earth (4:05)

4 Bigger (3:17)

5 One Less Lonely Girl (3:49)

6 First Dance (3:42)

7 Love Me (3:13)

8 One Less Lonely Girl [Video] [Multimedia]

9 One Time [Video] [Multimedia]

PUZZLE ANSWERS

SPOT THE DIFFERENCE

IN A SPIN

1. KATY PERRY

2. WILL FERRELL

3. CHERYL COLE

4. JADEN SMITH

5. KIM KARDASHIAN

6. TAIO CRUZ

BIEBER TRIVIA

Do you know everything there is to know about Justin? Could you outwit his own mum with your knowledge of the Bieb? Put yourself to the test with our tricky quiz . . .

1 WHAT COLOUR ARE JUSTIN'S EYES?

a. Blue

b. Green

c. Brown

2 WHAT IS JUSTIN'S DOG CALLED?

a. Benny

b. Sammy

c. Jerry

3 WHAT YEAR WAS JUSTIN BORN?

a. 1993

b. 1994

c. 1995

4 HOW OLD WAS JUSTIN WHEN HE STARTED PLAYING THE DRUMS?

a. Two

b. Three

c. Five

5 WHAT DOES JUSTIN SAY HIS WORST HABIT IS?
a. Burping
b. Eating too many sweets
c. Forgetting to change his socks

7 WHAT IS JUSTIN'S FAVOURITE SPORT?
a. Ice hockey
b. Baseball
c. Basketball

6 WHAT PHOBIA DOES JUSTIN HAVE?
a. Arachnophobia (fear of spiders)
b. Agoraphobia (fear of going outside)
c. Claustrophobia (fear of small places)

8 WHAT'S JUSTIN'S FAVOURITE SCHOOL SUBJECT?
a. Maths
b. English
c. Biology

9 WHAT'S JUSTIN'S PERSONAL MOTTO?
a. The best things in life are free
b. If you ain't first, you're last
c. The sun will come out tomorrow

10 JUSTIN IS...
a. Ambidextrous
b. Right handed
c. Left handed

HOW DID YOU SCORE?

0-3 BRUSH UP ON YOUR BIEBER
You're not that clued-up on Biebs just yet, but a little practice makes perfect.

4-6 BELIEBER
Good skills – you know lots about JB – but there's still a bit more to learn.

7-10 UBERBELIEBER
Wow, you know more about Biebs than mother Bieber herself!

Answers: 1 – c; 2 – b; 3 – b; 4 – a; 5 – b; 6 – c; 7 – a; 8 – b; 9 – b; 10 – c

MY GREATEST EVER BIEBER MOMENT

What better way to end the best Bieber book ever, than with a place to write down your fave Bieber experience to date? Over to you...!